AF470055

This book belongs to

AN ABC BOOK OF ENTREPRENEURS WHO CHANGED THE WORLD

ILLUSTRATIONS BY CARA JANE DIFFEY

Any reference contained in this book to celebrities or public figures does not constitute or imply the endorsement, recommendation or approval of those artists

is for

Adolf Dassler

Adidas

"A bad idea is always better than none at all.
Only by trying can the wrong become right"

is for

Bill Gates

Microsoft

"To win big, you sometimes have
to take big risks"

is for

Coco Chanel

Chanel

"In order to be irreplaceable, one must always be different"

is for

Diddy

Bad Boy Entertainment

"If you want to fly, you have to give up
the things that weigh you down"

is for

Albert Einstein

Physicist

"Imagination is more important than knowledge"

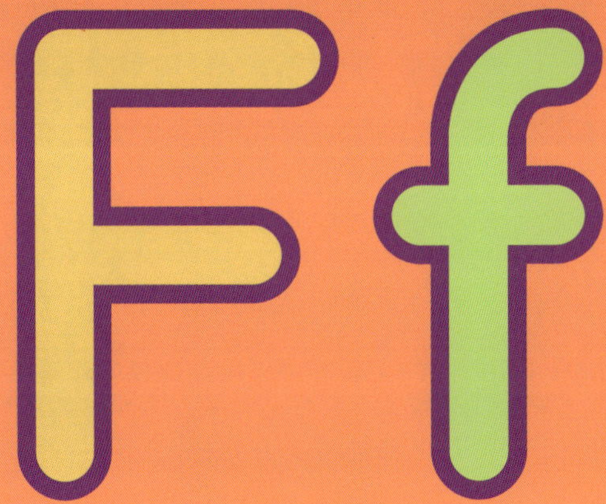

is for

Enzo Ferrari

Ferrari

"If you can dream it, you can do it"

is for

George Eastman

Kodak

"What we do during our working hours determines what we have; what we do in our leisure hours determines what we are"

is for

Henry Ford
Ford Motors

"When everything seems to be going against you, remember that the airplane takes off against the wind, not with it"

Ii

is for

Ingvar Kamprad
IKEA

"Happiness is not reaching your goal.
Happiness is being on the way"

J j

is for

J.K. Rowling
Harry Potter

"It is our choices that show what we truly are, far more than our abilities"

Kk

is for

Kevin Systrom

Instagram

"Do what you love, and do it well - that's much more meaningful than any metric"

Ll

is for

Larry Page
Google

"If you're not doing some things that
are crazy, then you're doing
the wrong things"

is for

Michael Jordan

Air Jordan

"Talent, teamwork and intelligence win championships"

Nn

is for

Nikola Tesla

Inventor

"One must be sane to think clearly, but one can think deeply and be quite insane"

is for

Oprah Winfrey
The O Network

"Surround yourself with only people who are going to lift you higher"

is for

Phil Knight

Nike

"Hard work is critical, a good team is essential, brains and determination are invaluable, but luck may decide the outcome"

is for

Quentin Tarantino

Director

"Don't write what you think people want to read. Find your voice and write about what's in your heart"

is for

Richard Branson

Virgin

"An entrepreneur is an innovator, a job creator, a game-changer, a business leader, a disruptor, an adventurer"

Ss

is for

Steve Jobs

Apple

"The people who are crazy enough to
think they can change the world
are the ones who do"

Tt

is for

Tom Ford
Tom Ford

"You have to love what you do, to the point that you cannot imagine doing anything else with your life. You have to sleep, breathe and live this"

is for

Uber

Travis Kalanick

"Go against the grain, be resilient, even if everyone thinks you are crazy"

UBER
UBER
UBER
UBER
UBER

is for

Gary Vaynerchuk

Vayner Media

"We only get to play this game one time. We have one life"

is for

Walt Disney

Disney

"If you can dream it, you can do it. Always remember that this whole thing was started by a mouse"

is for

Alexander Graham Bell
Inventor

"Before anything else, preparation is the key to success"

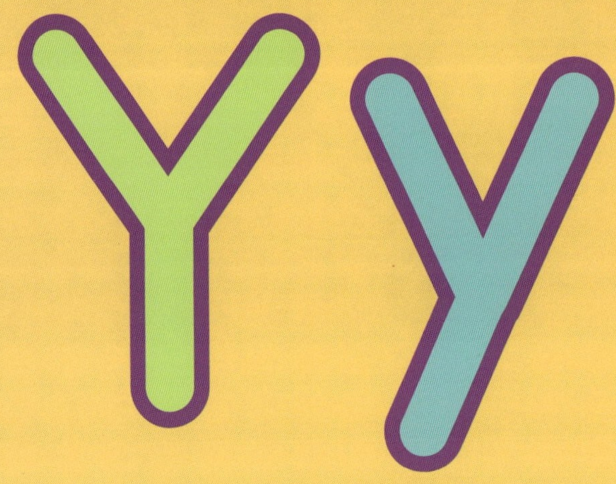

is for

Fusajiro Yamauchi

Nintendo

"Never go the easy path, always challenge yourself and try to do something new"

Zz

is for

Mark Zuckerberg

Facebook

"Some people dream of success, while
others wake up and work hard at it"